Forgotten
Passwords
Here

Kay D Johnson

Johnson, Kay D
Forgotten Passwords Here

ISBN 978-1-989194-50-8 (pkb)

GoMe! Publishing

Since this book holds all your private and valuable information, please keep this book in a safe place at all times.

A

Website:
Email:
User Name:
Password:
Security Question/Hint
Notes:

Website:
Email:
User Name:
Password:
Security Question/Hint
Notes:

Website:
Email:
User Name:
Password:
Security Question/Hint
Notes:

A

Website:
Email:
User Name:
Password:
Security Question/Hint
Notes:

Website:
Email:
User Name:
Password:
Security Question/Hint
Notes:

Website:
Email:
User Name:
Password:
Security Question/Hint
Notes:

A

Website:
Email:
User Name:
Password:
Security Question/Hint
Notes:

Website:
Email:
User Name:
Password:
Security Question/Hint
Notes:

Website:
Email:
User Name:
Password:
Security Question/Hint
Notes:

A

Website:
Email:
User Name:
Password:
Security Question/Hint
Notes:

Website:
Email:
User Name:
Password:
Security Question/Hint
Notes:

User Name:
Password:
Security Question/Hint
Notes:

B

Website:
Email:
User Name:
Password:
Security Question/Hint
Notes:

Website:
Email:
User Name:
Password:
Security Question/Hint
Notes:

Website:
Email:
User Name:
Password:
Security Question/Hint
Notes:

B

Website:
Email:
User Name:
Password:
Security Question/Hint
Notes:

Website:
Email:
User Name:
Password:
Security Question/Hint
Notes:

Website:
Email:
User Name:
Password:
Security Question/Hint
Notes:

B

Website:
Email:
User Name:
Password:
Security Question/Hint
Notes:

Website:
Email:
User Name:
Password:
Security Question/Hint
Notes:

Website:
Email:
User Name:
Password:
Security Question/Hint
Notes:

B

Website:
Email:
User Name:
Password:
Security Question/Hint
Notes:

Website:
Email:
User Name:
Password:
Security Question/Hint
Notes:

Website:
Email:
User Name:
Password:
Security Question/Hint
Notes:

| Website: |
| Email: |
| User Name: |
| Password: |
| |
| |
| Security Question/Hint |
| |
| Notes: |
| |

| Website: |
| Email: |
| User Name: |
| Password: |
| |
| |
| Security Question/Hint |
| |
| Notes: |
| |

| Website: |
| Email: |
| User Name: |
| Password: |
| |
| |
| Security Question/Hint |
| |
| Notes: |
| |

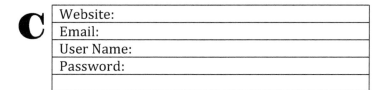

C

| Website: |
| Email: |
| User Name: |
| Password: |
| |
| |
| Security Question/Hint |
| |
| Notes: |
| |

| Website: |
| Email: |
| User Name: |
| Password: |
| |
| |
| Security Question/Hint |
| |
| Notes: |
| |

| Website: |
| Email: |
| User Name: |
| Password: |
| |
| |
| Security Question/Hint |
| |
| Notes: |
| |

C

Website:
Email:
User Name:
Password:
Security Question/Hint
Notes:

Website:
Email:
User Name:
Password:
Security Question/Hint
Notes:

Website:
Email:
User Name:
Password:
Security Question/Hint
Notes:

C

| Website: |
| Email: |
| User Name: |
| Password: |
| |
| |
| Security Question/Hint |
| |
| Notes: |
| |

| Website: |
| Email: |
| User Name: |
| Password: |
| |
| |
| Security Question/Hint |
| |
| Notes: |
| |

| Website: |
| Email: |
| User Name: |
| Password: |
| |
| |
| Security Question/Hint |
| |
| Notes: |
| |

D

| Website: |
| Email: |
| User Name: |
| Password: |
| |
| |
| Security Question/Hint |
| |
| Notes: |
| |

| Website: |
| Email: |
| User Name: |
| Password: |
| |
| |
| Security Question/Hint |
| |
| Notes: |
| |

| Website: |
| Email: |
| User Name: |
| Password: |
| |
| |
| Security Question/Hint |
| |
| Notes: |
| |

D

Website:
Email:
User Name:
Password:
Security Question/Hint
Notes:

Website:
Email:
User Name:
Password:
Security Question/Hint
Notes:

Website:
Email:
User Name:
Password:
Security Question/Hint
Notes:

D

Website:
Email:
User Name:
Password:
Security Question/Hint
Notes:

Website:
Email:
User Name:
Password:
Security Question/Hint
Notes:

Website:
Email:
User Name:
Password:
Security Question/Hint
Notes:

D

Website:
Email:
User Name:
Password:
Security Question/Hint
Notes:

Website:
Email:
User Name:
Password:
Security Question/Hint
Notes:

Website:
Email:
User Name:
Password:
Security Question/Hint
Notes:

E

Website:
Email:
User Name:
Password:
Security Question/Hint
Notes:

Website:
Email:
User Name:
Password:
Security Question/Hint
Notes:

Website:
Email:
User Name:
Password:
Security Question/Hint
Notes:

Website:
Email:
User Name:
Password:
Security Question/Hint
Notes:

Website:
Email:
User Name:
Password:
Security Question/Hint
Notes:

Website:
Email:
User Name:
Password:
Security Question/Hint
Notes:

Website:
Email:
User Name:
Password:
Security Question/Hint
Notes:

E

Website:
Email:
User Name:
Password:
Security Question/Hint
Notes:

Website:
Email:
User Name:
Password:
Security Question/Hint
Notes:

E

Website:
Email:
User Name:
Password:
Security Question/Hint
Notes:

Website:
Email:
User Name:
Password:
Security Question/Hint
Notes:

Website:
Email:
User Name:
Password:
Security Question/Hint
Notes:

F

Website:
Email:
User Name:
Password:
Security Question/Hint
Notes:

Website:
Email:
User Name:
Password:
Security Question/Hint
Notes:

Website:
Email:
User Name:
Password:
Security Question/Hint
Notes:

F

Website:
Email:
User Name:
Password:
Security Question/Hint
Notes:

Website:
Email:
User Name:
Password:
Security Question/Hint
Notes:

Website:
Email:
User Name:
Password:
Security Question/Hint
Notes:

F

Website:
Email:
User Name:
Password:
Security Question/Hint
Notes:

Website:
Email:
User Name:
Password:
Security Question/Hint
Notes:

Website:
Email:
User Name:
Password:
Security Question/Hint
Notes:

F

Website:
Email:
User Name:
Password:
Security Question/Hint
Notes:

Website:
Email:
User Name:
Password:
Security Question/Hint
Notes:

Website:
Email:
User Name:
Password:
Security Question/Hint
Notes:

G

Website:
Email:
User Name:
Password:
Security Question/Hint
Notes:

Website:
Email:
User Name:
Password:
Security Question/Hint
Notes:

Website:
Email:
User Name:
Password:
Security Question/Hint
Notes:

G

Website:
Email:
User Name:
Password:
Security Question/Hint
Notes:

Website:
Email:
User Name:
Password:
Security Question/Hint
Notes:

Website:
Email:
User Name:
Password:
Security Question/Hint
Notes:

G

Website:
Email:
User Name:
Password:
Security Question/Hint
Notes:

Website:
Email:
User Name:
Password:
Security Question/Hint
Notes:

Website:
Email:
User Name:
Password:
Security Question/Hint
Notes:

G

Website:
Email:
User Name:
Password:
Security Question/Hint
Notes:

Website:
Email:
User Name:
Password:
Security Question/Hint
Notes:

Website:
Email:
User Name:
Password:
Security Question/Hint
Notes:

H

Website:
Email:
User Name:
Password:
Security Question/Hint
Notes:

Website:
Email:
User Name:
Password:
Security Question/Hint
Notes:

Website:
Email:
User Name:
Password:
Security Question/Hint
Notes:

Website:
Email:
User Name:
Password:
Security Question/Hint
Notes:

Website:
Email:
User Name:
Password:
Security Question/Hint
Notes:

Website:
Email:
User Name:
Password:
Security Question/Hint
Notes:

H

Website:
Email:
User Name:
Password:
Security Question/Hint
Notes:

Website:
Email:
User Name:
Password:
Security Question/Hint
Notes:

Website:
Email:
User Name:
Password:
Security Question/Hint
Notes:

Website:
Email:
User Name:
Password:
Security Question/Hint
Notes:

Website:
Email:
User Name:
Password:
Security Question/Hint
Notes:

Website:
Email:
User Name:
Password:
Security Question/Hint
Notes:

I

Website:
Email:
User Name:
Password:
Security Question/Hint
Notes:

Website:
Email:
User Name:
Password:
Security Question/Hint
Notes:

Website:
Email:
User Name:
Password:
Security Question/Hint
Notes:

I

| Website: |
| Email: |
| User Name: |
| Password: |
| |
| |
| Security Question/Hint |
| |
| Notes: |
| |

| Website: |
| Email: |
| User Name: |
| Password: |
| |
| |
| Security Question/Hint |
| |
| Notes: |
| |

| Website: |
| Email: |
| User Name: |
| Password: |
| |
| |
| Security Question/Hint |
| |
| Notes: |
| |

I

Website:
Email:
User Name:
Password:
Security Question/Hint
Notes:

Website:
Email:
User Name:
Password:
Security Question/Hint
Notes:

Website:
Email:
User Name:
Password:
Security Question/Hint
Notes:

I

| Website: |
| Email: |
| User Name: |
| Password: |
| |
| |
| Security Question/Hint |
| |
| Notes: |
| |

| Website: |
| Email: |
| User Name: |
| Password: |
| |
| |
| Security Question/Hint |
| |
| Notes: |
| |

| Website: |
| Email: |
| User Name: |
| Password: |
| |
| |
| Security Question/Hint |
| |
| Notes: |
| |

J

Website:
Email:
User Name:
Password:
Security Question/Hint
Notes:

Website:
Email:
User Name:
Password:
Security Question/Hint
Notes:

Website:
Email:
User Name:
Password:
Security Question/Hint
Notes:

J

Website:
Email:
User Name:
Password:
Security Question/Hint
Notes:

Website:
Email:
User Name:
Password:
Security Question/Hint
Notes:

Website:
Email:
User Name:
Password:
Security Question/Hint
Notes:

J

Website:
Email:
User Name:
Password:
Security Question/Hint
Notes:

Website:
Email:
User Name:
Password:
Security Question/Hint
Notes:

Website:
Email:
User Name:
Password:
Security Question/Hint
Notes:

J

Website:
Email:
User Name:
Password:
Security Question/Hint
Notes:

Website:
Email:
User Name:
Password:
Security Question/Hint
Notes:

Website:
Email:
User Name:
Password:
Security Question/Hint
Notes:

K

Website:
Email:
User Name:
Password:
Security Question/Hint
Notes:

Website:
Email:
User Name:
Password:
Security Question/Hint
Notes:

Website:
Email:
User Name:
Password:
Security Question/Hint
Notes:

K

Website:
Email:
User Name:
Password:
Security Question/Hint
Notes:

Website:
Email:
User Name:
Password:
Security Question/Hint
Notes:

Website:
Email:
User Name:
Password:
Security Question/Hint
Notes:

K

Website:
Email:
User Name:
Password:
Security Question/Hint
Notes:

Website:
Email:
User Name:
Password:
Security Question/Hint
Notes:

Website:
Email:
User Name:
Password:
Security Question/Hint
Notes:

K

Website:
Email:
User Name:
Password:
Security Question/Hint
Notes:

Website:
Email:
User Name:
Password:
Security Question/Hint
Notes:

Website:
Email:
User Name:
Password:
Security Question/Hint
Notes:

L

Website:
Email:
User Name:
Password:
Security Question/Hint
Notes:

Website:
Email:
User Name:
Password:
Security Question/Hint
Notes:

Website:
Email:
User Name:
Password:
Security Question/Hint
Notes:

L

Website:
Email:
User Name:
Password:
Security Question/Hint
Notes:

Website:
Email:
User Name:
Password:
Security Question/Hint
Notes:

Website:
Email:
User Name:
Password:
Security Question/Hint
Notes:

L

| Website: |
| Email: |
| User Name: |
| Password: |
| |
| |
| Security Question/Hint |
| |
| Notes: |
| |

| Website: |
| Email: |
| User Name: |
| Password: |
| |
| |
| Security Question/Hint |
| |
| Notes: |
| |

| Website: |
| Email: |
| User Name: |
| Password: |
| |
| |
| Security Question/Hint |
| |
| Notes: |
| |

L

Website:	
Email:	
User Name:	
Password:	
Security Question/Hint	
Notes:	

Website:	
Email:	
User Name:	
Password:	
Security Question/Hint	
Notes:	

Website:	
Email:	
User Name:	
Password:	
Security Question/Hint	
Notes:	

M

Website:
Email:
User Name:
Password:
Security Question/Hint
Notes:

Website:
Email:
User Name:
Password:
Security Question/Hint
Notes:

Website:
Email:
User Name:
Password:
Security Question/Hint
Notes:

M

Website:
Email:
User Name:
Password:
Security Question/Hint
Notes:

Website:
Email:
User Name:
Password:
Security Question/Hint
Notes:

Website:
Email:
User Name:
Password:
Security Question/Hint
Notes:

M

Website:
Email:
User Name:
Password:
Security Question/Hint
Notes:

Website:
Email:
User Name:
Password:
Security Question/Hint
Notes:

Website:
Email:
User Name:
Password:
Security Question/Hint
Notes:

M

Website:
Email:
User Name:
Password:
Security Question/Hint
Notes:

Website:
Email:
User Name:
Password:
Security Question/Hint
Notes:

Website:
Email:
User Name:
Password:
Security Question/Hint
Notes:

N

Website:
Email:
User Name:
Password:
Security Question/Hint
Notes:

Website:
Email:
User Name:
Password:
Security Question/Hint
Notes:

Website:
Email:
User Name:
Password:
Security Question/Hint
Notes:

N

Website:
Email:
User Name:
Password:
Security Question/Hint
Notes:

Website:
Email:
User Name:
Password:
Security Question/Hint
Notes:

Website:
Email:
User Name:
Password:
Security Question/Hint
Notes:

Website:
Email:
User Name:
Password:
Security Question/Hint
Notes:

N

Website:
Email:
User Name:
Password:
Security Question/Hint
Notes:

Website:
Email:
User Name:
Password:
Security Question/Hint
Notes:

N

Website:
Email:
User Name:
Password:
Security Question/Hint
Notes:

Website:
Email:
User Name:
Password:
Security Question/Hint
Notes:

Website:
Email:
User Name:
Password:
Security Question/Hint
Notes:

O

Website:
Email:
User Name:
Password:
Security Question/Hint
Notes:

Website:
Email:
User Name:
Password:
Security Question/Hint
Notes:

Website:
Email:
User Name:
Password:
Security Question/Hint
Notes:

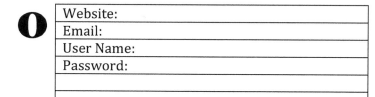

| Website: |
| Email: |
| User Name: |
| Password: |
| |
| |
| Security Question/Hint |
| |
| Notes: |
| |

| Website: |
| Email: |
| User Name: |
| Password: |
| |
| |
| Security Question/Hint |
| |
| Notes: |
| |

| Website: |
| Email: |
| User Name: |
| Password: |
| |
| |
| Security Question/Hint |
| |
| Notes: |
| |

Website:
Email:
User Name:
Password:
Security Question/Hint
Notes:

O

Website:
Email:
User Name:
Password:
Security Question/Hint
Notes:

Website:
Email:
User Name:
Password:
Security Question/Hint
Notes:

Website:
Email:
User Name:
Password:
Security Question/Hint
Notes:

Website:
Email:
User Name:
Password:
Security Question/Hint
Notes:

Website:
Email:
User Name:
Password:
Security Question/Hint
Notes:

P

Website:
Email:
User Name:
Password:
Security Question/Hint
Notes:

Website:
Email:
User Name:
Password:
Security Question/Hint
Notes:

Website:
Email:
User Name:
Password:
Security Question/Hint
Notes:

P

Website:	
Email:	
User Name:	
Password:	
Security Question/Hint	
Notes:	

Website:	
Email:	
User Name:	
Password:	
Security Question/Hint	
Notes:	

Website:	
Email:	
User Name:	
Password:	
Security Question/Hint	
Notes:	

P

Website:
Email:
User Name:
Password:
Security Question/Hint
Notes:

Website:
Email:
User Name:
Password:
Security Question/Hint
Notes:

Website:
Email:
User Name:
Password:
Security Question/Hint
Notes:

Website:
Email:
User Name:
Password:
Security Question/Hint
Notes:

Website:
Email:
User Name:
Password:
Security Question/Hint
Notes:

Website:
Email:
User Name:
Password:
Security Question/Hint
Notes:

Website:
Email:
User Name:
Password:
Security Question/Hint
Notes:

Q

Website:
Email:
User Name:
Password:
Security Question/Hint
Notes:

Website:
Email:
User Name:
Password:
Security Question/Hint
Notes:

Website:
Email:
User Name:
Password:
Security Question/Hint
Notes:

Website:
Email:
User Name:
Password:
Security Question/Hint
Notes:

Website:
Email:
User Name:
Password:
Security Question/Hint
Notes:

Website:
Email:
User Name:
Password:
Security Question/Hint
Notes:

Q

Website:
Email:
User Name:
Password:
Security Question/Hint
Notes:

Website:
Email:
User Name:
Password:
Security Question/Hint
Notes:

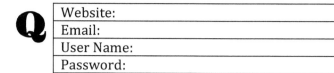

Website:
Email:
User Name:
Password:
Security Question/Hint
Notes:

Website:
Email:
User Name:
Password:
Security Question/Hint
Notes:

Website:
Email:
User Name:
Password:
Security Question/Hint
Notes:

R

Website:
Email:
User Name:
Password:
Security Question/Hint
Notes:

Website:
Email:
User Name:
Password:
Security Question/Hint
Notes:

Website:
Email:
User Name:
Password:
Security Question/Hint
Notes:

Website:
Email:
User Name:
Password:
Security Question/Hint
Notes:

Website:
Email:
User Name:
Password:
Security Question/Hint
Notes:

Website:
Email:
User Name:
Password:
Security Question/Hint
Notes:

Website:
Email:
User Name:
Password:
Security Question/Hint
Notes:

R

Website:
Email:
User Name:
Password:
Security Question/Hint
Notes:

Website:
Email:
User Name:
Password:
Security Question/Hint
Notes:

| Website: |
| Email: |
| User Name: |
| Password: |
| |
| |
| Security Question/Hint |
| |
| Notes: |
| |

| Website: |
| Email: |
| User Name: |
| Password: |
| |
| |
| Security Question/Hint |
| |
| Notes: |
| |

| Website: |
| Email: |
| User Name: |
| Password: |
| |
| |
| Security Question/Hint |
| |
| Notes: |
| |

S

Website:
Email:
User Name:
Password:
Security Question/Hint
Notes:

Website:
Email:
User Name:
Password:
Security Question/Hint
Notes:

Website:
Email:
User Name:
Password:
Security Question/Hint
Notes:

| Website: |
| Email: |
| User Name: |
| Password: |
| |
| |
| Security Question/Hint |
| |
| Notes: |
| |

| Website: |
| Email: |
| User Name: |
| Password: |
| |
| |
| Security Question/Hint |
| |
| Notes: |
| |

| Website: |
| Email: |
| User Name: |
| Password: |
| |
| |
| Security Question/Hint |
| |
| Notes: |
| |

Website:	
Email:	**S**
User Name:	
Password:	
Security Question/Hint	
Notes:	

Website:
Email:
User Name:
Password:
Security Question/Hint
Notes:

Website:
Email:
User Name:
Password:
Security Question/Hint
Notes:

S

| Website: |
| Email: |
| User Name: |
| Password: |
| |
| |
| Security Question/Hint |
| |
| Notes: |
| |

| Website: |
| Email: |
| User Name: |
| Password: |
| |
| |
| Security Question/Hint |
| |
| Notes: |
| |

| Website: |
| Email: |
| User Name: |
| Password: |
| |
| |
| Security Question/Hint |
| |
| Notes: |
| |

T

Website:
Email:
User Name:
Password:
Security Question/Hint
Notes:

Website:
Email:
User Name:
Password:
Security Question/Hint
Notes:

Website:
Email:
User Name:
Password:
Security Question/Hint
Notes:

T

Website:
Email:
User Name:
Password:
Security Question/Hint
Notes:

Website:
Email:
User Name:
Password:
Security Question/Hint
Notes:

Website:
Email:
User Name:
Password:
Security Question/Hint
Notes:

T

Website:
Email:
User Name:
Password:
Security Question/Hint
Notes:

Website:
Email:
User Name:
Password:
Security Question/Hint
Notes:

Website:
Email:
User Name:
Password:
Security Question/Hint
Notes:

T

| Website: |
| Email: |
| User Name: |
| Password: |
| |
| |
| Security Question/Hint |
| |
| Notes: |
| |

| Website: |
| Email: |
| User Name: |
| Password: |
| |
| |
| Security Question/Hint |
| |
| Notes: |
| |

| Website: |
| Email: |
| User Name: |
| Password: |
| |
| |
| Security Question/Hint |
| |
| Notes: |
| |

U

Website:
Email:
User Name:
Password:
Security Question/Hint
Notes:

Website:
Email:
User Name:
Password:
Security Question/Hint
Notes:

Website:
Email:
User Name:
Password:
Security Question/Hint
Notes:

U

Website:
Email:
User Name:
Password:
Security Question/Hint
Notes:

Website:
Email:
User Name:
Password:
Security Question/Hint
Notes:

Website:
Email:
User Name:
Password:
Security Question/Hint
Notes:

U

Website:
Email:
User Name:
Password:
Security Question/Hint
Notes:

Website:
Email:
User Name:
Password:
Security Question/Hint
Notes:

Website:
Email:
User Name:
Password:
Security Question/Hint
Notes:

U

Website:
Email:
User Name:
Password:
Security Question/Hint
Notes:

Website:
Email:
User Name:
Password:
Security Question/Hint
Notes:

Website:
Email:
User Name:
Password:
Security Question/Hint
Notes:

V

Website:

Email:

User Name:

Password:

Security Question/Hint

Notes:

Website:

Email:

User Name:

Password:

Security Question/Hint

Notes:

Website:

Email:

User Name:

Password:

Security Question/Hint

Notes:

V

| Website: |
| Email: |
| User Name: |
| Password: |
| |
| |
| Security Question/Hint |
| |
| Notes: |
| |

| Website: |
| Email: |
| User Name: |
| Password: |
| |
| |
| Security Question/Hint |
| |
| Notes: |
| |

| Website: |
| Email: |
| User Name: |
| Password: |
| |
| |
| Security Question/Hint |
| |
| Notes: |
| |

Website:	
Email:	
User Name:	
Password:	
Security Question/Hint	
Notes:	

V

Website:
Email:
User Name:
Password:
Security Question/Hint
Notes:

Website:
Email:
User Name:
Password:
Security Question/Hint
Notes:

V

Website:
Email:
User Name:
Password:
Security Question/Hint
Notes:

Website:
Email:
User Name:
Password:
Security Question/Hint
Notes:

Website:
Email:
User Name:
Password:
Security Question/Hint
Notes:

W

Website:
Email:
User Name:
Password:
Security Question/Hint
Notes:

Website:
Email:
User Name:
Password:
Security Question/Hint
Notes:

Website:
Email:
User Name:
Password:
Security Question/Hint
Notes:

Website:
Email:
User Name:
Password:
Security Question/Hint
Notes:

Website:
Email:
User Name:
Password:
Security Question/Hint
Notes:

Website:
Email:
User Name:
Password:
Security Question/Hint
Notes:

Website:	**W**
Email:	
User Name:	
Password:	
Security Question/Hint	
Notes:	

Website:
Email:
User Name:
Password:
Security Question/Hint
Notes:

Website:
Email:
User Name:
Password:
Security Question/Hint
Notes:

Website:
Email:
User Name:
Password:
Security Question/Hint
Notes:

Website:
Email:
User Name:
Password:
Security Question/Hint
Notes:

Website:
Email:
User Name:
Password:
Security Question/Hint
Notes:

X

Website:
Email:
User Name:
Password:
Security Question/Hint
Notes:

Website:
Email:
User Name:
Password:
Security Question/Hint
Notes:

Website:
Email:
User Name:
Password:
Security Question/Hint
Notes:

X

Website:
Email:
User Name:
Password:
Security Question/Hint
Notes:

Website:
Email:
User Name:
Password:
Security Question/Hint
Notes:

Website:
Email:
User Name:
Password:
Security Question/Hint
Notes:

X

Website:
Email:
User Name:
Password:
Security Question/Hint
Notes:

Website:
Email:
User Name:
Password:
Security Question/Hint
Notes:

Website:
Email:
User Name:
Password:
Security Question/Hint
Notes:

Website:
Email:
User Name:
Password:
Security Question/Hint
Notes:

Website:
Email:
User Name:
Password:
Security Question/Hint
Notes:

Website:
Email:
User Name:
Password:
Security Question/Hint
Notes:

Y

Website:
Email:
User Name:
Password:
Security Question/Hint
Notes:

Website:
Email:
User Name:
Password:
Security Question/Hint
Notes:

Website:
Email:
User Name:
Password:
Security Question/Hint
Notes:

Y

Website:
Email:
User Name:
Password:
Security Question/Hint
Notes:

Website:
Email:
User Name:
Password:
Security Question/Hint
Notes:

Website:
Email:
User Name:
Password:
Security Question/Hint
Notes:

Y

Website:
Email:
User Name:
Password:
Security Question/Hint
Notes:

Website:
Email:
User Name:
Password:
Security Question/Hint
Notes:

Website:
Email:
User Name:
Password:
Security Question/Hint
Notes:

Y

| Website: |
| Email: |
| User Name: |
| Password: |
| |
| |
| Security Question/Hint |
| |
| Notes: |
| |

| Website: |
| Email: |
| User Name: |
| Password: |
| |
| |
| Security Question/Hint |
| |
| Notes: |
| |

| Website: |
| Email: |
| User Name: |
| Password: |
| |
| |
| Security Question/Hint |
| |
| Notes: |
| |

Website:	
Email:	
User Name:	
Password:	
Security Question/Hint	
Notes:	

Website:
Email:
User Name:
Password:
Security Question/Hint
Notes:

Website:
Email:
User Name:
Password:
Security Question/Hint
Notes:

Website:
Email:
User Name:
Password:
Security Question/Hint
Notes:

Website:
Email:
User Name:
Password:
Security Question/Hint
Notes:

Website:
Email:
User Name:
Password:
Security Question/Hint
Notes:

Z

Website:
Email:
User Name:
Password:
Security Question/Hint
Notes:

Website:
Email:
User Name:
Password:
Security Question/Hint
Notes:

Website:
Email:
User Name:
Password:
Security Question/Hint
Notes:

Website:
Email:
User Name:
Password:
Security Question/Hint
Notes:

Website:
Email:
User Name:
Password:
Security Question/Hint
Notes:

Website:
Email:
User Name:
Password:
Security Question/Hint
Notes:

≪ NOTES ≫

＜ NOTES ＞

≪ NOTES ≫

≪ NOTES ≫